THE TALISMAN

THE TALISMAN

The Autobiography of Marcel Dassault

Creator of the Mirage Jet

TRANSLATED BY PATRICIA HIGH PAINTON

ARLINGTON HOUSE, *New Rochelle, New York*

CONTENTS

6

PREAMBLE

Throughout my career, I've often been asked, and still am asked even now, "What kind of a man are you, Mr. Dassault?"

After all, it's a perfectly normal question. In my lifetime, I've managed to succeed in quite a few undertakings. The aircraft I have created bear the names which I chose especially for them—names that make people dream. My planes fly throughout the world, and everywhere, they are the best testimonials to their own qualities.

So the question also means, "How have you succeeded, Mr. Dassault?"

There is, I think, a simple answer to that. Without false modesty, I would say that I've always made a special effort to use my imagination. With the team of men I trained, I've worked hard. I don't allow myself to become discouraged by difficulties. I have a passion for my work, and I know how to use my will power to brush aside anything which might distract me from it. Everything in my surroundings must be geared to the great work I've assigned myself.

Of course, like every human being, I've had my share of pain and suffering. But it is neither in my character nor in my approach to life to allow misfortune to upset my plan. What plan? Achievement. Achievement of what? Everything that my reason and my dreams together have shown to be both necessary and possible.

My nature, the importance of my work—everything leads me to give brief answers to questions to which I know the answer. By instinct, I don't answer the others.

Since people who question me find my answers a bit short, they sometimes add something of their own to what I've said and end up, in effect, answering for me.

Well, everyone knows how anecdotes are born and how those people who tell them like to embroider the facts for the sake of a better story in a conversation.

My friends know that, thanks to my Marseillaise mother, I have a cheerful nature and tend towards optimism. But I am, I admit, uncommunicative. The basis of my character is reflectiveness, at the core of which is an ability to foresee what might happen in order to be ready for any eventuality.

My company is a happy place where work is done with pleasure. I am interested in the well-being of those around me. I'm never unaware for long of my colleagues' disappointments or pleasures. I have my share of these ups and downs, and over the years events have proven that we all are bound to each other by ties which are very real, even if we don't talk about them much.

The result is that there is hardly any turnover on my staff. I still have the same men working with me that I've always had. Those who came later have been integrated into the original team.

What's more, none of us has forgotten men like Rozanoff and Bigand, just to mention those two, who, while working with us on a day that seemed like any other day, were to give all that a man can give. Their sacrifice has given our work an aspect which is both special and, even, let me say, sacred.

I like drawing. My family always had a predilection for the arts. My cousin is the world-renowned musical composer Darius Milhaud.

When I was a child, my mother often used to take me to visit her aunt, the Countess of Camondo, who was the sister of her mother. It was in this magnificent Camondo mansion, along the edge of the Parc Monceau in Paris, where I learned to know and appreciate painting, sculpture and rare art objects. My cousin, Nissim de Camondo, died for France during the 1914–18 war, and in his memory, his father made a gift of the mansion with all the art works it contained to the city of Paris. It is now the Museum Nissim de Camondo, 63, Rue de Monceau.

I love the rich silence where, for me, another kind of music is born—the music of great tasks and endeavors in which you can hear the singing of the future. It is this music I chose, not because I did not know how to appreciate the other, but because my kind of music is necessary to me, while the other is merely a pleasure.

I like to read, and I've read a great deal. Assuming I had to go off to live on a desert island, as in that old parlor game, I would bring along the works of La Fontaine where I find everything anyone could want—morality, wisdom, poetry, fantasy, and also the great lessons in politics which André Siegfried discussed so well. I would also take with me the writings of Madame de Segur, since my whole life has been influenced by those years when I was such an attentive young reader of hers. This good and charming lady has more to teach than appears.

But this is enough for a preamble. I have grouped under chapter headings those questions I'm most often asked, and I've tried to answer them as I went along.

Here, then, is the kind of man I am, since that is the question which appears to be of interest. I answer it directly but not without a certain embarrassment because for me, too, self-revelation is painful.

MY FAMILY

I was born in Paris, at 47 Rue Blanche, of an Alsatian father and a Marseillaise mother.

My father was a doctor. He was already an intern at the Hospital of Paris at the time of the siege of 1870. His great hobby was anthropology, and he was later elected President of the Anthropological Society. But his true calling was medicine, and you can understand his dedication when you realize that he either walked or took a bus to make his many house calls—climbing countless stairs on each visit, since in those days elevators were practically non-existent.

A doctor who is devoted to patients of modest means is rarely able to think of himself or add to his estate. My father was no exception.

Then, too, the devaluations of the currency which followed the First World War meant that when his life of dedication ended, he was completely destitute.

What is there to say about a loving mother except that she was wonderful?

We were four brothers. The oldest died young. The second was General of the Army Dassault, Grand Chancellor of the Legion of Honor, and member of the Academy of Sciences. He distinguished himself during the resistance movement against Nazi Germany, serving at the secret headquarters of the group called the "Francs-Tireurs et Partisans." He also received the Médaille Militaire and the Croix de Guerre with numerous clusters. The third brother was a surgeon at the Hospital of Paris, Officer of the Legion of Honor and also held the Croix de Guerre with numerous clusters. During the war he was deported to Germany, where he died.

I am an aeronautical engineer. Thus we four brothers all chose different careers.

We were born at five-year intervals and we were always ready to help each other. There was never even the slightest argument between us. Each of us was proud of his own success and happy with the success of the others.

My start in life took place in the square of the Church of the Trinity, bordered by Rue Blanche and Rue Clichy.

It was a period when we played games like tag and prisoner's base.

THE LYCÉE

Once, when I was in the seventh grade, I received the best marks in the class for drawing and recitation. My parents were proud of me and offered to give me a present of my own choice. After a long search through many stores, I suddenly stopped in front of a set for electrical experiments. This was in 1902. The Exposition of 1900 had shown Parisians some of the marvels of electricity, but the benefits of this new power source were still not widely known, and for light, people used oil and gas. It wasn't the way it is now when children can choose among countless electric and electronic toys.

This electricity set, however, was not really

a toy but in fact a small laboratory for electrical experiments. There was, for example, a Ruhmkorff coil and a Geissler Tube—the kinds of things you don't find in the electric and electronic toys children play with today.

I became fascinated with electricity and later added on to this first electricity set. That was how I acquired my first Crookes Tube, which produces X-rays, and I used to amuse myself by taking photographs of keys inside a cardboard box.

My parents were happy to see me become interested in this new science and my friends at the time were amazed at the experiments I was able to conduct for them.

I was very impressed by the life of Edison who had started as a newsboy and became a great inventor, scientist and industrialist.

When I was in the ninth grade, around 1906, I had an idea one day based on my new awareness of the possibilities of science. I reasoned that if Edison could record the human voice through a groove made on a wax cylinder, it should be possible to record also through a metallic wire which, by passing in front of an electro-magnet, would receive magnetic waves in direct proportion to the intensity of the human voice. Essentially, that was the tape recorder.

Unfortunately, at the time I completely lacked the means to develop this idea, and subsequently I became interested in other problems. Forty years later, I learned that during World War II the Americans had developed the tape recorder on an industrial basis. Since then the invention has spread throughout the world.

Because I was always more interested in practical matters than in classical studies, my parents gave me permission to enter an electrical engineering school, l'École Bréguet, at the Rue Falguière.

At that time the school taught at a vocational training level, so my studies were as much practical as they were theoretical. Each week we took three hours of industrial design and three hours of shopwork which included work with the bench vice and practicing with various machine tools like lathes and drills.

During recreation period one day when I was in the courtyard of the school, I saw an airplane go by for the first time. It was a Wilbur Wright plane, owned by the Count of Lambert, and it was circling the Eiffel Tower.

Although they were Americans, the Wright brothers tested some of their first airplanes in France.

Since the Rue Falguière wasn't very far

from the airfield at Issy-les-Moulineaux, I often used to go to see those first airplanes fly. There were planes like the "Demoiselle" of Santos-Dumont and many others.

It was to honor Antoine Bréguet that our school director, Mr. Schneider, decided to name the school after that pioneer of electrical engineering.

The ancestor of Antoine Bréguet, Abraham Bréguet, was a clockmaker from Neuchatel, in Alsace, who came to Paris in the 18th century and was appointed clockmaker to the royal court. His great grandson, Antoine Bréguet, was a great electrical engineer whose work took place at the very beginnings of the new science.

The children of Antoine Bréguet, in their turn, changed directions completely and became aircraft manufacturers. It was in one of their planes that Coste and Bellonte made the first East-West crossing of the Atlantic.

On graduation day at the school I received my diploma as an electrical engineer from the hands of Louis Bréguet. I was nineteen at the time and, of course, I never dreamed that one day I would become the major stockholder in the Bréguet Aviation Company.

A TRAINING PERIOD IN A FACTORY

During the long summer holidays which followed I took a job as a trainee in the Panhard
automobile factory. After working at various
stages of the production I reached the point
where the finishing touches were being put on
the big 24-horsepower, valveless automobiles.

My work consisted of tuning the motor and
then road-testing the chassis, the seat being
nothing more than a tool chest.

It was there that I first observed how a
big heavy machinery plant operated. I also
learned to appreciate the labor of the workers,
their team spirit and their pleasure when the
company won a race, broke a record or brought
out a successful new model car.

THE ÉCOLE SUPÉRIÉURE D'AÉRONAUTIQUE

After the École Bréguet, I decided to enter the École Supérieure d'Aéronautique, which had been established two years earlier by Colonel Roche. He had managed to engage very eminent men in various fields to teach the subjects. Thus Paul Painlevé, who is often overlooked as primarily a great mathematician, gave a course on the mechanics of fluids.

Colonel Renard himself taught the science of dirigible balloons. He was the brother of that other Colonel Renard who had built the dirigible "France", which was so famous at that time. A street in Paris in the 17th arrondissment is named after these two scientist brothers.

Major Dorant, director of the Aeronautical Laboratory, gave us a course in propellers.

MILITARY SERVICE

The time for military service had come. Former students of the École Supérieure d'Aéronautique had the right to enter directly into the aviation regiments of the Corps of Engineers and I thought I would be able to complete the technical education I'd received so far in school by an extended study of military aircraft prototypes.

After three months of classes at Reims I was detached to the Aeronautical Laboratory at Chalis-Meudon, which was under the command of my former teacher, Major Dorant.

The laboratory was divided into different sections in which Major Dorant's colleagues—all officers—were studying the entire range of technical problems connected with aeronautics.

Thus Major Dorant himself worked on experimental aircraft while Major Saconnet constructed kites to be used for observation, and Captain Lelarge built mobile hydrogen pumps for reinflating balloons while in the field, etc.

THE CAUDRON G-3

Then came the war of 1914–18.

There were quite a few aircraft manufacturers in existence already, notably Blériot, who had flown the English Channel; Deperdussin, who had broken the closed circuit speed record by reaching 200 kilometers per hour. Farman, Voisin, Morane, Saulnier, Caudron—all these manufacturers' names were known to the public through the feats of the aircraft they had made.

General Hirschauer, who was in charge of aviation at the Ministry of War, decided to limit the number of models of planes to be built. For bombers he chose Voisin, for fighter planes, Morane, and for reconnaissance, Farman and Caudron.

The manufacturing of each model was divided up among the different companies so that all the existing means of production at that time could be used to the fullest.

It was in this way that the Blériot factory, the SPAD factory and two Caudron factories were assigned to manufacture the G-3 reconnaissance aircraft.

As sometimes happens with a company and its subcontractor, relations between Caudron and Blériot were far from perfect. Blériot, for instance, complained that the design studies for the Caudron G-3 were not adequate. Captain Etévé, who was in charge of constructing the Caudron G-3s, asked Major Dorant to send him an engineer from the Aeronautical Laboratory who could improve the design studies and also coordinate the manufacture of the G-3s in the four factories.

I was the one chosen.

Captain Etévé let me know I would have a lot of work to do, since the Blériot plant was in Suresnes, the SPAD plant at Rue des Entrepreneuers in Paris and Caudron itself had just moved into two new factories, one at Issy-les-Moulineaux and the other at Lyon. He asked me if I had a friend who could work with me on polishing up the design studies and coordinating the manufacturing. I proposed my friend Henry Potez, who had graduated a year ahead of me at the École Supérieure d'Aéronautique and who also was working in the Aeronautical Laboratory with me. Captain Etévé agreed and so Potez came to work with me.

After the final preparation of the design studies of the Caudron G-3, we handled the coordination of the manufacturing of the planes in the four factories. We also made some modifications in the planes, which had been suggested by pilots at the front. For example, the whole lay-out of the fuselage was changed so that the pilot's seat was shifted to the machine-gunner's seat and vice versa.

Our relationship with both Caudron and Blériot was very good and they were very happy with our work.

Captain Etévé also was highly pleased with our performance. I was promoted from Corporal to Sergeant and Potez became a Corporal. Later we both reached the rank of Second Lieutenant at the same time.

FLIGHT TESTING
THE FARMAN F–40S

Once the G-3s had been built, Potez was taken on as a designer at the Design Department of Caudron at Lyon, and I was transferred to flight testing the Farmans at Buc, under the orders of Captain Cassin. My job consisted of flying with the pilots and then later writing up a report on the performance and flying characteristics of each plane.

That was how I got to know Maurice Farman who often took me with him on his flights. Above all he loved to fly at tree-top level and underneath our F–40 we could watch the rabbits and partridges scatter in the fields which, at that time, teemed with game because hunting was forbidden during the war.

The personal plane of Maurice Farman had been fitted out with great care, but it was a long way from the comfort of the Mystère 20 which I use for my travelling today.

Flight testing the Farmans left me with some leisure time, and, knowing that the propeller of the Caudron could be improved upon, I decided to build a better propeller. But to explain how I was able to do that I'll have to go back a few years.

THE "HELICE ECLAIR"

When I went into the eighth grade I was full of a sense of my own importance. After all, I'd just left the little Lycée Condorcet at the Rue Amsterdam, which went as far as the seventh grade, and I was entering the big Condorcet Lycée at the Rue Caumartin. In effect I was leaving childhood behind and entering adolescence.

On the first day of class I arrived ahead of time and picked out a seat in the front row right next to the door. Was it to get out of the classroom quicker at recess? I don't remember the reason anymore. At any rate I had put down my briefcase at the seat I'd chosen and then gone for a walk in the lycée courtyard to get an idea of the layout of the new school.

When I returned to the classroom I found somebody else's briefcase where mine had been and my briefcase pushed further along the row. I put my briefcase back where it was and sat down at the place I'd chosen.

When the intruder came back he shoved me, and a fight was just getting under way when the teacher arrived. I stayed in my place and the other boy sat down next to me. We had wanted to sit in the same seat, probably because we had the same tastes. Later we became close friends

The other boy was Georges Hennequin who later became a brilliant architect. He had a friend, Marcel Hirch, and we three became an inseparable trio.

My friend Marcel Hirch had a charming young sister who later was to become my wife. His father, Mr. Hirch, was a former upholsterer. He was very intelligent, hard-working and full of common sense.

In the old days when young people were married they used to order their living room furniture especially made from an upholsterer. It took so long to be made that sometimes these newly-married couples had time to get divorced before they finally were able to furnish their living room.

Mr. Hirch was the first to mass produce

Aubusson-style furniture, making exact repro-
ductions of the kinds of pieces you can see in
national museums like those at Fontainebleau
and Chantilly. He would get the wooden
frames carved for him and then gild and deco-
rate the rest himself, at least in the early part
of his career. Then he would cover the pieces
with Aubusson tapestry made by the artisans
of the Creuse. These living room suites had a
great success and his company grew rapidly.

Since I completely lacked the means to build
the propeller I had in mind, I went to Mr.
Hirch for help. He liked people to be bold and
enterprising so he agreed to put a skilled carpenter at my disposal along with some planks
of hard wood. I made the design of my propeller, then traced sections of it onto the wood so
that the carpenter could follow the outlines. I
stayed right at his side while he planed down
the propeller, guiding his hand along the har-
monious lines I was trying to achieve.

Once the propeller was finished a name had
to be found for it. It was called the "Éclair"
propeller.

I asked Blériot for permission to have it
tested at Buc by one of his pilots. Since it was
found to be very satisfactory, I presented it to
the Villacoublay Testing Center. This propel-

ler was rated the best, and the company, "Helice-Eclair," was given an initial contract for fifty of them. The price of each one amounted to about 150 francs at that time.

To organize the production of the first order, which was followed by many others, I was transferred to "Helice-Eclair." I was beginning to have more work than I could handle so I asked Potez to come with me. He quit the Design Department at Caudron without regret. We built these propellers for many other types of planes: the Sopwith, which was a British reconnaissance plane built under license in France, the Doran AR, which meant "avant Renault" to distinguish it from the Farman which had a Renault engine at the rear, and in a few months we became one of the four biggest propeller manufacturers of that time. We outgrew the workshops of Mr. Hirch, and all the furniture makers of the Faubourg Saint-Antoine were put to making "Eclair" propellers.

It was at this time, in 1916, that I built the propeller for the French ace Guynemer whose SPAD, called "Le Vieux Charles," had chalked up 19 kills and now is kept at the Invalides Museum as a war memorial.

HOW TO BECOME AN AIRPLANE MANUFACTURER

Having graduated from the École Supérieure d'Aéronautique, I knew aviation technology.

I became familiar with design and manufacturing by having coordinated the production of the Caudron G-3 at Blériot and Caudron, and also through having made the final design drawings of the plane and even changing some of these designs.

What I still lacked was a knowledge of flight testing and the final preparation of an aircraft.

As it turned out, the construction of propellers was the best possible training for becoming an aircraft manufacturer.

Aircraft manufacturers confided to the propeller builders all the characteristics of their planes: the weight, the wing span, power of the engine, etc. Starting with that information, the propeller constructor had to calculate the diameter, the profile, and the torque of his propeller in order to get the best performance from the plane—speed, rate of climb, etc.

Thus I came to know the characteristics of all the planes being constructed at that time. I followed their development from the moment they were conceived until their final preparation in order to make sure that my propellers were functioning correctly. I was continually visiting airfields carefully noting down the little mishaps that occurred with either a plane's engine or body and how these problems were later ironed out.

That was how I learned the techniques of flight testing and the final preparation of a new aircraft.

Having learned which new models succeeded and which ones failed, I was able to acquire a great deal of experience in deciding what should and should not be done to make a good airplane.

What's more, I noted that at that time a good two-seater fighter plane just did not exist, and that's where I got the idea of building one.

THE S.E.A.
FIGHTER PLANE

Potez and I were not directly connected with the company which was manufacturing our propellers. We just received a kind of licensing fee based on the company's total sales. But with this income, along with our savings, we were able to build our two-seater fighter plane, S.E.A. 4, around 1917. At that time the government did not finance the construction of prototypes, which had to be done at the expense of the manufacturers.

Potez and I had formed a small company called "Société d'Études des Aéronautiques," standing for S.E.A. 4. Potez was a very good engineer, an excellent businessman and a discerning financier. He taught me a lot of things during that period which stood me in good stead in later years.

But before we could build the plane we first had to design it.

One of my classmates from the École Supérieure d'Aéronautique called Coroller worked in the Defense Ministry, at the Boulevard des Invalides. We rented from him the small bachelor's apartment where he was living. It was located at the back of a courtyard in a building on Rue Constantine, and every night from nine o'clock to midnight Potez, Coroller and I went there to work on the design of our plane.

Later Coroller was to become the Technical Director of the Société des Aéroplanes Henry Potez.

Once the plans were completed we rented a small factory at Suresnes, hired a foreman and a few workers and constructed our airplane.

The two-seater fighter plane was equipped with a 375-horsepower Lorraine engine. It was first tested by our pilot, Douchy, one of the aces of the 1914–18 war, later by pilots from the Flight Testing Center at Villacoublay and finally by combat pilots at the front.

By the time all these tests were completed, it was already the end of 1917.

A thousand of these planes were ordered.

Naturally, they were not supposed to be manufactured in our little factory in Suresnes, but under our direction in all the factories of all the big companies and sub-contractors of that time. At that point I was 26 years old and Potez was 27. It was a pretty good start.

Only a few of these planes were built by the time of the armistice in 1918. The war which we had won at such a high cost in human lives was regarded by everyone then as "the war to end all wars". The government services responsible for airplane production informed us that, if we wished, we could make doors, windows or wheelbarrows, but it would be a long time before any new orders for aircraft were given. And even if someday a government order were to be given, it would be for only a few airplanes, and it would go to the big companies with big factories and reserves of manpower, like Voisin, Bréguet, Farman and others.

DIVERSIFICATION

After the 1918 armistice certain big aircraft companies tried to diversify. For example, Blériot started making boats, and Voisin, automobiles. For my part, having only a small amount of capital, I turned toward housing construction.

Just before the war, the city of Paris extended the Avenue Ledru-Rollin all the way to the Place Voltaire. On either side of that avenue there still were plots of land for sale. I knew about them because they were in the same neighborhood as the furniture makers where we had constructed our "Éclair" propellers.

I bought three of these small lots on which

I then built commercial buildings. Once they were up they were rented quickly to furniture manufactuers, and I earned a good income from them. But at the same time I had used up my available capital and in order to continue in this new field, I needed either to find associates or to borrow more capital.

I decided on the latter course, and I built a number of buildings both for commercial use and as dwellings, which I sold by individual apartments. The venture into real estate ended up happily but like some promoters today, I sometimes had difficulties.

This difficult period in my career taught me a great many things which many people who have the luck (or bad luck) to succeed too early and too fast never are able to learn.

In 1930, twelve years after the armistice, all the aircraft manufacturers who had diversified into other fields more or less had suffered setbacks. I was about the only one to succeed in converting to other activities.

THE PROTOTYPE POLICY

Around 1930 the government began to wake up to the fact that other countries, especially Germany, were making great progress in aviation. Since the Germans were not allowed to build airplanes under the terms of the armistice, they had created big aircraft plants in Sweden. Britain, America and Italy too were making progress.

Italy's advances were particularly noted one day when a squadron of Italian seaplanes commanded by Marshal Balbo crossed France and completely left behind the squadron of Nieuport fighters which had been sent up to intercept them.

In France various manufacturers were producing planes, but they were all very similar to those of the late war. Moreover, transport aviation was in its infancy.

The government realized that to make progress in aviation and to avoid being outdistanced by neighboring countries, an Air Ministry had to be created.

Mr. Laurent-Eynac was the first Minister of Air and Mr. Caquot became the Technical and Industrial Director General of the ministry.

Albert Caquot, an engineer of the Corps des Ponts-et Chaussées, is one of the great men of our times. We owe to him the George Vth bridge in Glasgow, the reconstruction of the port of Saint-Nazaire and the dam at Donzère-Mondragon. He is also one of the best aviation technicians of all time. He was a man who looked to the future in everything he did.

He therefore decided on a national aviation policy which consisted of ordering prototypes of modern airplanes from already-existing aircraft companies. At the same time, he gave certain engineers who had left the field of aviation the opportunity to return to it.

I knew Mr. Caquot personally since he had been the director of technical services in the Ministry of War during the 1914–18 war and he remembered very well my "Éclair" propeller as well as the two-seater fighter plane, the S.E.A. 4. I went to see him. He received me very warmly and offered me a contract for the prototype of a three-engine postal courier.

I accepted and immediately went to work laying down the general characteristics of the plane. Having noted that planes made of wood and canvas were increasingly out of date, I decided to make my plane entirely of metal and with thick wings.

To work out the plans for this aircraft I needed a design department, and so I first of all hired an engineer, Riffard, whom I knew well. He came from the Lioré et Olivier company and later was to leave me to become the Technical Director of Caudron-Renault where he created all their prototypes, in particular one aircraft which won the Deutsch de la Meurthe cup.

To complete the design department I then hired several more engineers who had answered the want ads I had placed in the newspapers. That was how Mr. Vallières, later President and General Director of the Avions Marcel Dassault, came to my company and also Henri Deplante who was to become Technical Director.

I had no factory at my disposal at that time

and so I had the plane built in the plant of a manufacturer of airplane gas tanks while my engineers and I oversaw the production. The plane first was tested at Buc by a brilliant pilot, Delmotte, whom Mr. Blériot was kind enough to put at my disposal. It was then tested by the pilots of the Flight Testing Center at Villacoublay.

It was far from being a failure. In fact if the truth be told, it was ranked first in the air show of the time. But Mr. Caquot was ahead of his time. Postal aviation was not really to get under way until twenty years later, and my beautiful prototype, even though successful, did not earn any production orders.

Mr. Caquot's prototype policy proved successful since the prototypes he chose along the lines he had laid out were the ones manufactured in the future period he had foreseen so precisely.

While I was following the tests of my three-engine postal plane at the Flight Testing Center at Villacoublay, I discovered that the flying ambulances which had been ordered for the evacuation of wounded were not very successful and could be improved upon.

At that time all the available government credit for prototypes had been used up, but since a flying ambulance was small and not very expensive to build I decided to make one without any government help.

With the capital from the sale of one of my buildings on Avenue Ledru-Rollin I rented a small factory in Boulogne and installed a few machines in it.

I still had my design department which had been used to work up the plans for the three-engine postal plane.

All I had to do was to hire a foreman and about a dozen workers.

In six months I built the plane entirely of metal, using the techniques learned from the three-engine postal plane. After an extremely rapid final preparation the aircraft was presented to the Flight Testing Center at Villacoublay. It was judged to be far superior to its competitors and earned a production order for twenty more. Later these planes were used in the campaigns in Syria and Morocco.

In order to meet the production order for the flying ambulances and also to work on other prototypes I rented a bigger factory at Courbevoie. Enough time having elapsed, the Ministry of Air once more had credit available for prototypes, and I was given an order for a three-engine plane to be used in the colonies which was little more than a modification of the earlier postal plane.

This plane was also a success. I received a production contract for twelve of them. Six were used by the Army air force in the colonies and six others were put to use as civil transport planes on the Algiers-Brazzaville-Madagascar line, which was run by Commandant Dagnaud. These planes gave complete satisfaction.

Wanting to do something for our big national airline, Air France, I built, at my own expense, the prototype of a twin-engine civil transport plane, the 220, with a capacity of carrying 16 passengers, a pilot and a mechanic. It was equipped with two Gnôme–et–Rhône engines, each with 1,000 horsepower.

Around ten of these planes were used by Air France. They went into service in 1938. It was in one of these planes that Daladier went to Munich while Chamberlain used a much slower Lockheed model. The 220s stayed in service throughout the German occupation and one or two of them still were being used two years after the armistice in 1945.

I also built a twin-engine bomber, the 210, the successor to the twin-engine Lioré 220 biplane, along with the fighter plane 150, which was a competitor of the Morane 406.

THE MODERN PLANES
GO INTO SERVICE
IN 1939

After Munich it was decided to equip the Air
Force with modern planes.

Since aircraft were becoming more and
more complicated and expensive to construct,
it was also decided to give up the air shows
which always resulted in orders for several
prototypes of the same kind of plane. Instead,
new aircraft were to be ordered from those
manufacturers whose technical capabilities
made them most likely to succeed.

That was how Dewoitine received a contract
for a fighter plane equipped with a 950-horse-
power Hispano engine, Lioré–et–Olivier got
the order for a bomber equipped with two
Gnôme–et–Rhône 1,000-horsepower engines,

and I was awarded the order for a reconnaissance plane also equipped with two Gnôme-et–Rhône 1,000 horsepower engines. That was the 174.

Unfortunately only a small number of these planes had been produced by September 1939 when the war broke out. They were all excellent planes, equal or superior to those of the enemy. The 174, especially, was probably the best aircraft of that period.

In October 1939 it was decided to produce two hundred 174s per month or 2,400 per year. But it took a year of preparation to produce the first 200, and after nine months the Battle of France was over.

If these planes had been ordered two years earlier at the same rate of production there would have been more than a thousand of each type available at the outbreak of the war, and that might have changed a lot of things. But, of course, a democracy in peacetime is just not able to indulge in such vast military expenditure.

Hitler, on the other hand, had been able to launch aircraft production at a wartime rhythm ever since 1936. He did not even bother to hide it. Goering used to take pleasure in showing off his factories and stocks of aircraft to foreign visitors, probably intending to discourage any government which might have wished to resist Nazi ultimatums.

The country which prepares for war, determined to attack at a time and place of its own choosing, always has the advantage over those countries which can only endure aggression.

Before the war I had built a four-engine civil transport plane, the "Languedoc 161," which also could be used as a troop carrier. It was the biggest French transport plane of that time. On its maiden flight it took off from Villacoublay and landed at Mérignac just as the Germans were entering Paris. But the Germans did not stop there, and when they reached Mérignac they found my four-engine plane and shipped it to Germany. After testing it there, the Germans wanted to use the plane as a troop transport and decided to have 100 of them constructed by Sud-Aviation at Toulouse.

The engineers and workers at Sud-Aviation managed to stall things so well that these planes still were not ready for delivery by the time the armistice was declared in 1945. Later, one hundred of them were produced. Fifty were assigned to the Navy and the other fifty were put into service by Air France for several years.

MY ARRIVAL AT BUCHENWALD

After the debacle of the defeat I found my way to the southern, unoccupied part of France where I often used to receive indirect offers from the Germans—transmitted through third persons—to work for them in the aviation industry. Naturally, I refused.

I was arrested at Lyon and deported to Buchenwald. On arriving at the assembly ground of the camp where the 40,000 prisoners were counted each morning and evening, I noticed a tall brick chimney. It was so hot the bricks glowed red, and it was giving off a thick, black and greasy smoke. I asked a veteran of the camp what was being burned in that chimney. He told me it was the crematorium, and that when you were in Buchenwald the big question was whether you would leave by the gate or by the chimney.

The camp included a big factory where components for the V–1 and V–2 rockets were made. Probably the reason the Nazis sent me to Buchenwald was to work in this factory. But three days before my arrival the Americans bombed and completely destroyed the factory. Seven hundred deportees and Nazi S.S. troops died together. The result was that the crematorium was working a little harder than normal that day, and as for me, I was not forced into helping the manufacture of V–1s and V–2s.

After leaving the assembly ground the newly-arrived prisoners were sent to take showers. First, all packages and clothes had to be left in a room, then we proceeded into a huge shower room. We left by a different door from the one we had entered through. We were given striped pants and jackets and, barefoot, we started off toward our new destiny.

My group was brought into a housing block, a kind of hangar, where 1,000 deportees lived. This hangar was divided into two rooms, one on the left, the other on the right, each housing five hundred men. Every block had a prisoner as its commander. Ours was a Pole. Each room also had its chief. The chief of the room to which I was assigned was Marcel Paul. He received us with kindness, and to our great astonishment, he told us the latest communiqué from the Free French Radio in London, "The French Speak to the French." Right away that was a great comfort to us.

In the manufacture of the V–2s there were a great many electronic components involved, and a talented prisoner had stolen enough of them to put together a radio. Of course, if he had been caught he would have faced the most serious punishment along with all those deportees who passed along news from the British radio broadcasts.

The S.S. guards lived outside the camp, which was run by the three prisoners who had been there the longest. These men were German Communists who had been in the camp since 1933. As the camp grew with the influx of political prisoners, these directors of the camp gave the Communists from various countries the key positions in their administration. That was how Marcel Paul became a Room Chief.

Marcel Paul was born in 1900. He was a child of the public welfare system. He began his career as an electrician with the Compagnie Parisienne de Distribution d'Électricité. Starting off as a member of the company's local union, he became its secretary-general and finally in 1932 he was elected the Secretary-General of the national union, the Federation of Public Services.

In 1941, while hiding out from the Germans, he took part in an abortive attempt to assassinate Goering. He was caught and deported to Buchenwald. With Manhès, he organized two secret groups. One combat group was to lead the fighting in case there was a prisoners' revolt or else a need to intervene with force as allied troops liberated the camp. The other group was responsible for advising the French prisoners on what attitude to take toward the SS and also to protect them, if necessary, without their even knowing it.

After the Liberation Marcel Paul became a member of the Constituent Assembly during a two-year period, 1945–46, then Minister of Industrial Production in the governments of de Gaulle, Gouin, and Bidault.

Finally, as President of the National Federation of Resisting and Patriotic Deportees and Internees, of which he was one of the founders, he even today continues to administer this association with the greatest devotion.

I won't describe to you the fate of the Buchenwald deportees because others have done it before me. Instead I'm going to tell you some anecdotes, some of them rather funny.

FRANCE OCCUPIED BY THE FRENCH

The deportees were allowed to write their families once a month. One day I saw several deportees writing letters. So I wrote one myself. When I wanted to give it to the chief of the block to send he said, "I can't send your letter because France is occupied." For him we were "occupied" by our own forces, helped by those of our American and British allies.

This expression of France being occupied by the French put me in a wonderful mood. Only those deportees whose countries were really occupied by the Germans were able to write to their families, and that included the Poles, the Rumanians, the Russians, the Belgians, the

Dutch, the Czechoslovaks, the Yugoslavs, the Greeks and many others.

No more work could be done at Buchenwald since the factory had been destroyed, and therefore my first concern was to stay there rather than be sent to another camp with a factory; to Dora, for instance.

THE DYSENTERY BLOCK

In my block there was a French doctor with a twin brother, also a doctor, who worked in the block reserved for dysentery patients. I asked this doctor to send me to his brother's block. He told me that he would do it the next morning and that I would be listed as sick by Roger Bellon, the famous founder of the pharmaceutical company of the same name, who was working with him as a male nurse. Roger Bellon promptly listed me as sick and that was how I entered the dysentery block. Other deportees had thought of the same idea with the result that there were many of us there. But we ran the risk of catching dysentery ourselves because there were many real dysentery cases there and people died from the disease every day.

Later the French doctor was replaced by a Czechoslovakian who did not take long to see through our ruse and send us back to our respective blocks.

I AM RECOGNIZED BY AN S.S. DOCTOR

Each month we underwent a kind of review inspection to see which of us still were capable of working. An S.S. doctor whom I did not know but who knew me, looked me over and said, "That's the French Junker. It's stupid to leave him in a deportee camp. He should be sent to work in a factory." I was very flattered to be called the French Junker because, although I had built some transport planes, Junker, on the other hand, was a very big German plane manufacturer.

Several weeks later, I was called to the tower —that is, to the residence of the S.S. troops outside the camp. Gathered there were the representatives of the German Air and Labor

Ministries. They had come to Buchenwald to look for certain workers to establish a new factory, and they told me I would be the director.

I pretended then that, not knowing how to speak German, I would not be able to direct a factory. They assigned me an interpreter on the spot.

My interpreter and I, along with two hundred deportees, were brought to a place called the departure block. We left the regular blocks where we lived and assembled in the departure block where we kept ready to leave at any hour of the day or night for an unknown destination.

DIPHTHERIA

Seizing on a moment when the chief of the block was looking elsewhere, I left to find Marcel Paul. I told him that up to now I had successfully avoided working for the Germans and I had no intention of starting at this point. I asked him to send me to the infirmary. He agreed to do it, and when I returned from the infirmary three or four days later, the departure block was completely deserted. Everybody had left and I was able to return to my old block, number 61.

There was, however, a problem. While at the infirmary I had caught diphtheria. Now this disease, caused by microbes, causes layers of skin to grow inside the throat and can bring death by strangulation. If you survive, which I did, you still aren't through with microbes. I learned later that they secrete a poison which attacks the nervous system. The first nerves affected are those of the soft palate with the result that when you drink, the liquid escapes through the nose, which is a very disagreeable sensation.

Some time later, after I had returned to France, I suffered a post-diphtheria paralysis of the legs. In the initial phase of this crisis the legs lose all their strength and you can no longer stand on them.

A few days before the camp was liberated the Germans decided to send by road to Austria all those prisoners they still felt could be useful to them. I was picked to leave and found myself lined up with the others when a prisoner wearing an arm-band—indicating his rank of camp policeman—said to me, "Follow me. You are under the protection of the Communist Party." The chief of the block did not object to my leaving the group and so I left with the camp policeman and he brought me to another block which the Germans had already checked over for useful and able-bodied prisoners to send to Austria. This meant that I was able to wait there for the three days before

the liberation of the camp. This camp policeman was from the group created by Manhès
and Marcel Paul to protect French deportees.

I was already suffering from the first symp-
toms of the post-diphtheria leg paralysis and if
I had left in the convoy then going on foot to
Austria, it's obvious that I would have fallen
along the roadside, and everyone knows what
happens in that case.

The Caudron G-3.

Captain Guynemer in front of his SPAD XIII equipped with an Eclair propeller.

Trimotor postal plane, Type 61.

The S.E.A. IV.

Colonial trimotor, Type 120.

Type 161 Languedoc.

MD 315 Flamant.

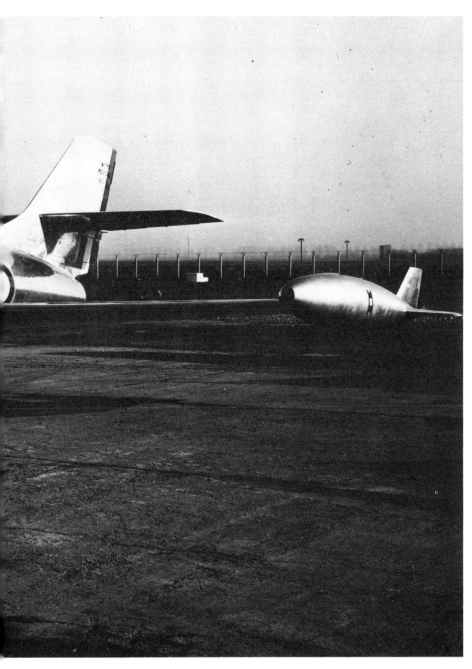

The Ouragan—first French jet.

The Super Mystère B-2.

Mystère IV

Mystère IV used by the Patrouille de France acrobatic flying team.

Mirage G with wings swept back for supersonic flight.

Mirage III-B.

Mirage III-C with Matra 530 air-to-air missile.

Mirage III-E fitted with a Nord AS 30 missile.

Spanish version of the Mirage III-EE.

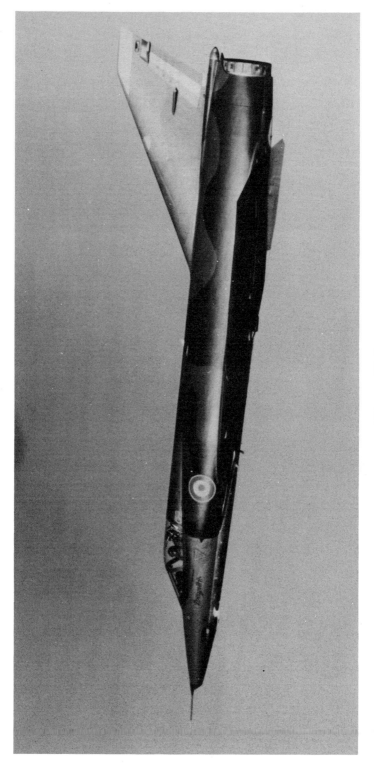

Mirage III-R.

Four versions of the Mirage: III-E, III-C, III-B, and III-R.

Australian version of the Mirage III-O.

Mirage IIIs of the South African Air Force.

Mirage IV.

The first three Mirage F-1s

Mirage V provided with 14 bombs.

Peruvian Mirage V-BP.

Belgian Mirage V-BA.

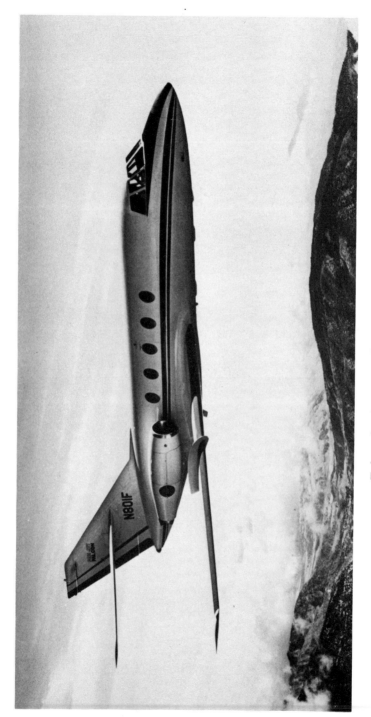

Falcon business jet above California.

Falcon 10 business jet.

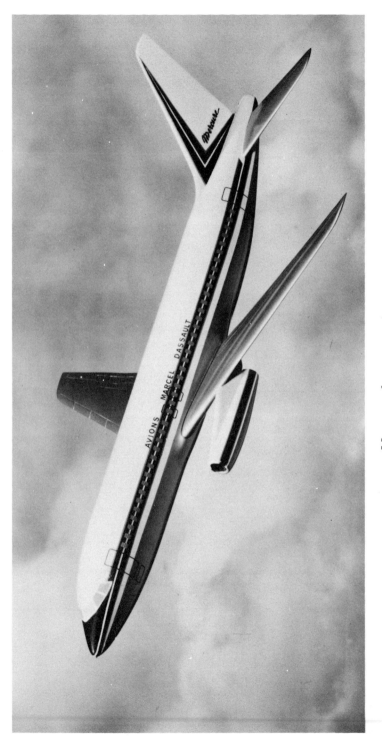

Mercure short-range jet.

Mercure 01.

Marcel Dassault at his desk.

THE LIBERATION

The day of the liberation of Buchenwald we all gathered together at the assembly grounds—this time without the S.S.

All of us—French, Russians, Poles, Slovaks, Czechs, Germans, Spaniards, Italians, Austrians, Belgians, Dutch, Luxemburgers, Rumanians, Yugoslavs, Hungarians—we all heard the oath of Buchenwald, delivered the 19th of April, 1945, and ending with these words:

"On these scenes of Fascist crimes, we swear before the whole world to continue the struggle until the last of those responsible has been condemned by the court of all the nations. We owe this to our fallen comrades and to their families.

"Our goal is the final crushing of Nazism. Our ideal is the building of a new world in peace and liberty.

"Raise your hands and swear to show that you are ready for the struggle."

Then the 21,000 survivors, lifting their arms, cried out in every kind of language:

"We swear it."

The German deportees among us kept their word because today the German Federal Republic is a democratic country like others.

THE RETURN

While a group of allied officers was visiting Buchenwald I asked a French officer if he had any news of my brother. He told me that General Dassault had just been named Grand Chancellor of the Legion of Honor by General de Gaulle.

We were supposed to leave the camp by plane, but there was a real threat of delay because there were so many people to evacuate.

A friend of Roger Bellon, a reserve officer who happened to be in Germany, had come to bring Bellon back to France with him by automobile. Roger Bellon invited me to come back with him. Rather than wait for a plane, other deportees also were finding ways to leave by car, and we left in a convoy of several cars.

Our first stop was Erfurt, the city where the heads of government of the two Germanies met for the first time. We were delighted by the charm of this extremely neat little town where we were invited to lunch by Baron Rothschild who was serving in the American Army at the time with the rank of Colonel. We took two days to get as far as the Rhine, which we crossed on a pontoon bridge, and finally reached Strasbourg.

We gathered together on the Place Kléber there and didn't quite know what to do. But our deportee uniforms quickly attracted a crowd of people hoping to get news from us of their deported relatives. We answered them the best we could. Then one of us suggested that, if we had the money, we all should go to the barber because we all had three- or four-day growths of beards. Right away the people who had been questioning us rushed to give us their small change. Then we went to the barber, but when the time came to pay he refused to accept our money. It was already late and we then went to ask for rooms at the Hotel de la Maison Rouge where the welcoming service for deportees had reserved rooms for us.

After that we thought the quickest way to

return to Paris would be to take a plane we hoped to find at the Strasbourg airfield, and that was how we returned on a three-engine Junker transport plane.

The plane was piloted by a French captain who knew me, and since I knew nothing of what had happened to my family while I was in Buchenwald, I asked the pilot to telegraph ahead to my brother at the Grand Chancellery of the Legion of Honor to advise my family of my arrival at Le Bourget airport, and that's how I came home at last.

AVIATION FROM 1945 TO THE PRESENT DAY

A few days after my return to France I suffered another attack of my post-diphtheria paralysis of the legs which required a six-month treatment.

To keep myself amused during this period of enforced idleness, I started designing a new liaison plane equipped with two 700 horse-power, 12 cylinder engines which I knew S.N.E.C.M.A. had built during the occupation.

Later this plane was to become the "Dassault 315."

I've always established the characteristics of my planes myself, working out the length of the fuselage, the wingspread, the weight per square meter of flying surface, the position of the tail unit, the type of engines, and so forth.

I've always closely followed the manufacture and final preparation of my planes. When the time comes for flight testing, I analyze the impressions of the test pilots in order to improve the plane's stability and also to make it more responsive to the controls and easier to handle.

When the war was definitely over with the surrender of Japan, Vallières and Deplante, who had joined the paratroopers in Britain and been through some hard fighting, came back to me to report for work.

During the war most of the factories had been bombed and disorganized. However, at the start of the war, while considering the construction of a new factory, I'd been lucky enough to order the metal framework for a building from a very conscientious contractor. He had managed to hide this framework throughout the occupation and was ready to deliver it to me.

So I went ahead and bought some land at Mérignac on which I put up this framework and thus found myself suddenly at the head of a modern factory located at an airfield.

Two years later I was in a position to bring out the twin-engine liaison plane, the "Dassault 315", which once again was ranked first in its class. Three hundred of these planes were ordered, and the production was divided up as follows: The fuselage went to the Société Nationale de Construction Aéronautique de Sud-Est et Toulouse; the wings were made at Nantes by the Société Nationale de Construction Aéronautique du Sud-Ouest, and the tail assembly was handled by Morane at Ossun.

It was the Société des Avions Marcel Dassault which drew up the central plane, handled the overall assembly and the flight tests.

Then came the first jet plane, the "Ouragan," which in the opinion of the pilots deserved its name and was greatly appreciated by the Air Force. Its speed was .75 Mach.

Finally I brought out the Mystère IV which was the first European plane to break the sound barrier. It won an "off-shore" contract from the Americans, meaning that following Marshall Plan policy, the Americans ordered and paid for 240 of these planes which then were handed over to the French Air Force as a gift. Mr. Pleven, Minister of National Defense at the time, complimented me in front of the National Assembly for having created the first aircraft in Europe to break the sound barrier, which also earned an "off-shore" contract.

Then there was the Super-Mystère B-2 and finally the Mirage III which opened the era of Mach 2 aircraft.

Next came the F-1, even more sophisticated than the Mirage III, and finally the swing-wing, single jet Mirage G which earned glowing reports from the Flight Testing Center, the military pilots at Mont-de-Marsan, and from American Air Force and Navy pilots who came over to test it.

As a result of the successful tests of the swing-wing, single jet Mirage G, I was given a contract for two twin-jet, swing-wing G-8s. The first one flew in Spring 1971.

At the same time I built a civil aircraft, the business jet, Mystère 20.

Now, we are building a smaller plane, the Mystère 10, which will be equipped with Larzac jet engines built by S.N.E.C.M.A., and a short-haul transport plane for 130 passengers, the Mercure, equipped with two Pratt & Whitney engines. Air Inter already has an option for ten of these transports and is thinking of ordering 30.

These three planes—the twin-jet, swing-wing G-8, the business jet Mystère 10, and the twin-engine, short-haul transport, the Mercure—were presented at the Salon du Bourget in June 1971.

MIRAGE III
AND MYSTÈRE 20

If all my planes have been successful, there are two models of which I am especially proud. One is the fighter-bomber, the Mirage III, and the other is the business jet, Mystère 20, known as the Fan Jet Falcon in the U.S.

The Mirage III was ordered by Mr. Chaban-Delmas when he was Minister of National Defense in 1957.

The first order for the French Air Force was for 90 planes. Later more than 1,200 of them were built, of which 300 went for France and the rest for exports to the rest of the world. Among those exported, it should be noted, were sixty Mirage IIIs which in the hands of Israeli pilots, proved their incontestable superiority during the Six-Day Mideast War.

The first Mystère 20, built at the expense of the Société des Avions Marcel Dassault, was exhibited at the Salon of 1965. Lindbergh, the famous pilot who crossed the Atlantic alone for the first time, had become the technical adviser to Pan American Airways. He noticed the Mystère 20, found it soundly designed and particularly well-built. He recommended the purchase of this plane to Pan American Airways which became the exclusive agent in the U.S. for the Société des Avions Marcel Dassault. In order to market the planes Pan American created the Business-Jet Corporation.

Thus 300 Mystère 20s were sold by the company in America while the Société des Avions Marcel Dassault on its own sold more than 100 others to 22 different countries on five continents.

So you could also say now that the sun never sets on the wings of a business jet Mystère 20. That was the way the Société des Avions Marcel Dassault became the foremost French exporter.

THE NAMES: MYSTÈRE, MIRAGE, AND MERCURE

I'm often asked about the origins of the names of my planes. Actually, in my childhood, I particularly loved to read the books of Paul d'Ivoi who was a writer in the vein of Jules Verne. His best-known work is *The Five Pennies of Lavarède*. But he also wrote another book entitled *Doctor Mystère*.

This fictional doctor had all kinds of unheard-of electronic devices. That was how he was able to install a screen which allowed him to see everything happening in the world; for example, the Carnival at Rio, the election of a President in the U.S., the 14th of July parade at Longchamps, etc. This book was written around 1900, and therefore foresaw the panoramic radar which could see through clouds and beyond hills.

It was in memory of the book *Doctor Mystère,* which had so fascinated me in my childhood, that I named my first supersonic plane the Mystère.

I named my Mirage III plane mirage because of the plane's qualities of attack and evasion, its ability to escape enemy thrusts most of the time.

"The Mirage is as invulnerable to the enemy's blows as the desert mirage is elusive to the desert traveler."

As for the Mercure, I wanted to give it the name of a god in Greek mythology, and finding only one with wings on his helmet and wing flaps on his feet, I called it Mercure.

THE ORGANIZATION OF THE SOCIÉTÉ DES AVIONS MARCEL DASSAULT

When I became a deputy in the National Assembly in 1951 I ceased being the President and General Director of the Société des Avions Marcel Dassault. That job now belongs to Mr. Vallières, an engineer from the École Supérieure d'Aéronautique and a paratrooper during the war, who has shown himself to be a marvelous industrialist and an excellent businessman, gifted with all the necessary technical ability. It is he who bargains with the government as well as with suppliers and who determines the salaries of the personnel.

My Technical Director is Henri Deplante, who also went to work for me upon graduating from school. He is an engineer from the École

Centrale des Arts et Manufactures and also was a paratrooper during the war.

We usually meet Saturday afternoons, myself, Vallières, Deplante, my principal engineers from the testing center, and the pilots. We talk about the final preparation of our planes and new projects to be developed. It works so well that I never lose contact with the top executives of my company. Whenever there is a factual error it is immediately corrected without recrimination because all are capable of making that kind of mistake.

My son Serge also attends these meetings as President and General Director of Electronique Marcel Dassault.

MY ACHIEVEMENTS IN SOCIAL BENEFITS

I've always attempted to improve the living conditions of my employees. That's why in 1935 I gathered together the union delegates at my plant in Courbevoie and offered to allocate 20 percent of the company's profits to the employees. They answered first by thanking me very much but then by saying they did not want to collaborate with the management, that they wanted to own the factory themselves and when that day came they would hire me as director because I was a good boss.

Since 1959 all my employees have participated in the prosperity of the company through a system whereby one percent of the total sales is divided up based on a coefficient which takes into account the value of each employee's contribution.

Thus I went back to the idea I'd had in 1935 to associate the employees with the success of the company but without bringing them into the responsibility of management, which is something they wanted nothing to do with.

It was also in 1935 that I decided to grant the employees of the Société des Avions Marcel Dassault a week's paid vacation, which was accepted with great satisfaction.

When Premier Léon Blum gave two weeks of paid vacation to French workers in 1937, representatives of my employees pointed out that the week's vacation I'd already granted them amounted to an acquired right to which must be added now the legal two weeks of vacation, thus giving them the right to a total of three weeks' vacation. I told them I agreed, and so my workers had three weeks of vacation during the last ten or fifteen years while other workers had only two weeks.

When the government gave three weeks' vacation to everybody my employees got four weeks.

Many years later, when Renault gave four weeks' vacation to its workers, I planned to pay all my employees by the month instead of by the hour, and that system now has been in effect for the last three years.

Besides enjoying a month's vacation, it's obvious that an employee paid by the month escapes from the basic proletarian situation through finding a greater degree of job security and a closer relationship with the company.

Most of the people who come to work for my company don't leave it until they retire. Most of them have five, ten, fifteen, twenty or thirty years of service, which means that given the extra day of vacation for every five years of service, they receive one, two, three, four, five or six days of extra vacation every year. Thus in addition to the four weeks of summer vacation, this year many of my employees will use their extra vacation time to take an eight-day winter holiday.

INDUSTRIAL AND TECHNICAL CAPACITIES

The little factory of 5,000 square meters at Mérignac, built in 1947, has grown. Today it covers 50,000 square meters.

Other factories have been added to this first one; those at Talence, de Martignas, Saint-Cloud, Boulogne-sur-Seine, d'Argenteuil, Villaroche, Istres, Annecy, etc. Altogether, these plants add up to 500,000 square meters.

The small design department of only three engineers now has grown into a design department of one thousand employees.

In addition to production of aircraft in its own plants, the Société des Avions Marcel Dassault provides work for various French companies like: the Société Nationale Industrielle

Aérospatiale, Latécoère, Potez, Hurel-Dubois, etc. And abroad we have furnished work to Fiat in Italy, the C.A.S.A. in Spain and to the S.A.B.C.A. in Belgium. In cooperation with Dornier in Germany we are making a twin jet trainer and close support aircraft, the Alpha-Jet.

Moreover, different types of Dassault planes have been built entirely under license in countries like Switzerland, Australia, South Africa, and so forth.

Since 1947 the Société des Avions Marcel Dassault has constructed 3,300 aircraft of all types.

Today it can be said that the prototypes mass-produced in my own factories, in addition to those built by sub-contractors and by licensees in foreign countries, provide work for more than 60,000 people.

THE NATIONAL ASSEMBLY

Until I was sixty years old I had actually never been in politics. I had my membership cards to the Radical Party and the Radical-Socialist party. I voted regularly for the Radical candidate in my local area without ever knowing him or asking him for anything.

In 1951 I received some advice from my friend General Corniglion-Molinier, a hero of the two wars, Grand Cross of the Legion of Honor, Companion of the Liberation, Médaille Militaire, Croix de Guerre, and a man always full of spirit, wit and charm. He told me, "General de Gaulle is going to launch a movement, 'the Rassemblement du Peuple Français'. This movement must get the maximum number of its followers elected to parliament so that someday General de Gaulle can return to power. I'm going to be a candidate, so you can be one too."

I followed this advice and became a deputy. After General de Gaulle became President of the Republic there was no longer any reason for me to remain a deputy, but since my constituents faithfully continue to re-elect me on the first round of voting, I've remained in parliament hoping to be useful to them.

A PARLIAMENTARY BILL

In June 1951 I became a member of the Committee on Reconstruction and a month later, I submitted a bill to allow people of modest means to become houseowners. This bill had been signed by several friends in my own political group as well as some friends in other groups, notably my friend Mr. Eugene Montel, a Socialist deputy and President of the General Council of the Haute-Garonne.

This bill provided for:

1) The establishment of several standard plans for the construction of houses of three, four, and five rooms.
2) The mass production of different mechani-

cal housing elements such as central heating, bathrooms, electric installations, kitchens, doors, windows, houseframes, etc.

3) Subsidies for housing construction and family housing allotments.

4) Contributions on the part of employers to the housing of their employees through a regular subscription of one percent of their total sales.

This bill was presented to the Committee on Reconstruction which assigned a chairman to it. This man was, perhaps, not exactly diligent because the bill has still never come up for discussion before the National Assembly.

A few years later Mr. Courant, then Minister of Reconstruction, was able to get a bill passed which provided for standard house plans, subsidies for housing construction and family housing allotments.

Subsequently, Mr. Laniel, then Prime Minister, had a law passed providing for the contribution by employees of a sum equal to one percent of their total payroll in order to provide credit for home buying.

I'm very happy that at least some of my ideas, first presented in my bill of 1951, were able to be taken up later and voted by the parliament. I'm only sorry, however, that so much time was wasted because home ownership by people of modest means is an essential element of human happiness and social justice.

JOURS DE FRANCE

Every parliamentarian wants to have a small newspaper. That is why General de Bénouville and I created *Jours de France*.

At the outset *Jours de France* was a political paper, but we very quickly realized that for a political journal to have any influence it had to be read widely, and for that, it had to avoid talking about politics.

This led us to create a mass circulation weekly in which we never talk about the catastrophes you see on television, hear on the radio and which finally are taken up by all the daily newspapers. We wanted to give our readers something different.

Women are very interested in romantic

fiction and above all in the fashion pages which also appeal to the men.

It's a weekly in which life is seen through rose-colored glasses.

Whenever by chance we publish an article on politics, it is seen by four million men and women readers.

THE TALISMAN

People tell me sometimes: "You have worked very hard, you have succeeded, but you also have been very lucky. People say you have a talisman."

I don't believe in good luck charms but I do believe in Providence. I'm going to tell you what my talisman was.

During the summer vacation in 1939, just before the war, I was walking in a field and discovered a four-leaf clover which I put in my wallet. I've already told you how on my arrival at Buchenwald we left our baggage, our clothes and everything we possessed before going into the shower room from which we emerged with only canvas coats and pants.

About three months after my return to Paris from deportation, I received a letter one day from the Minister of War Veterans and Former Deportees, asking me to come to a certain office to pick up some of my belongings. The office was on the Avenue-Bugeaud. To my great surprise I was given back my watch, my fountain pen, my wallet, which I signed for. Inside my wallet was still my four-leaf clover.

I consider that to find a four-leaf clover in Paris which I'd been forced to leave in Buchenwald, is, to say the least, a favorable sign from Providence. Perhaps it is in that sense that my four-leaf clover deserves to be called a talisman.

And that is the story of Marcel Dassault.

I've written this book thinking of the young. I wanted to show them that you don't have to inherit wealth to succeed—that you can do it by persevering. After all, even if everybody does not have his own four-leaf clover, each one at least has his own star.